The Darkest Secret of Life

The Darkest Secret of Life

By

Sheilah Nyakane

Copyright Sheilah Nyakane 2016

The Darkest Secret of Life

The Darkest Secret of Life

Published by

William Jenkins
2503 4288 Grange Street
Burnaby BC V5H 1P2
Canada

williamhenryjenkins@gmail.com
http://williamjenkins.ca

Cell: 1-778-953-6139

ISBN: 978-1-928164-17-3

The Darkest Secret of Life

The Darkest Secret of Life

My name is Sheilah Nyakane. I'm 18 years of age and I'm doing grade 12. I always dreamed to be a doctor but as I grew up, I began to be more interested in Law. I want to be an advocate or magistrate or a psychologist. I'm a girl with ambition. I always aim high even if I know what I aim for is impossible. You know why? It's because I always tell myself that the word impossible does not exist in my dictionary

The Darkest Secret of Life

I'm the first born of my family. I'm a sister to twins, a girl and boy. I'm living with my mom, a single parent who works very hard for the three of us.

Since I was 15, I've wanted to be a successful young author. I always wrote short stories on my scribbler, gave them to my mom and she would say 'you could go far if you follow this'. When I was 17 I decided to follow my ability and strength. I enjoy writing but I can sometimes be discouraged if anyone finds my writing boring.

I have two special friends who help me become the person I am. Palesa Shingange and Mixo Shiluvana are 19 and also doing grade 12. I met Palesa three years ago, She played a major role since then and she's still playing it today. Last year was a hard year for me. Each time I fell down, she picked me up. She really supported me. In times of tears, she wiped them away and put a big smile on my face. She has done so many things in my life. I thought of mentioning her because she appreciates the person I am. As for Mixo, I met her this year, but it feels as though I've known her for many years. She also plays a role in my life. She's so funny to have around. No matter how angry I may be, as long as she's around my anger fades away. I appreciate the kind of person she is in my entire life. I love these friends with all my heart and I pray to God to grant them the desires of their hearts.

The Darkest Secret of Life

The Darkest Secret of Life

Chapter One

"I don't know whether I should let it go or continue with the whole saga", I said to Marianne, my best friend.

"My friend, I suspect that your mother has a good reason why she doesn't want to discuss it with you".

I was mystified about my predicament at home. My mother kept a secret from me. She did not want to tell me about my father.

Marianne and I sat on a low, stone wall that marked the front of a café that served as a hangout for high school students from our school. I wasn't ready to join the crowd in the café. I wanted to get this worry out in the open and Marianne, thankfully, was willing to listen.

It's tough when your best friend is also the prettiest, most popular girl in the class. Smart as a whip, she would be able to cut through all the lies and give me the kind of advice I needed. She had her hair in a ponytail and her beautiful brown eyes matched the khaki jersey and short shorts she sported. Next to her, I felt a little drab, a little overweight and very much in need of some encouragement.

The Darkest Secret of Life

For the past sixteen years, information about my father had been kept from me. I always wished to meet him. I always asked about my father when I spoke with people who were close to my mother, but they did not give me any details of the kind I wanted. People would say 'We do not want to lie. Ask your mother. Maybe she has better answers for your questions'. Those replies would tear my heart apart, but I could not do anything about it.

It was not that I was the only student being raised by a single mother. There were several others in my class who had to scrape by to survive. However, they all knew about their parents; how a divorce had split them, how an unexpected sudden death had put them in a single parent category. I seemed to be the only one who had to live with the mystery about my father, perhaps never knowing my true heritage.

One winter day, I woke up in a very good mood and prepared for school. I did not know what put me in such a jovial mood that morning. When I finished preparing for the day, I waited for the bus to school as usual. As a 16-year-old teenager hoping to meet my father some day, I did not see anything unusual about the features of those who seemed to resemble me a little. I thought it was normal to look a little like someone who was not even a relative. I didn't search the streets for that special someone whom I resemble. I believed

The Darkest Secret of Life

that if my father existed, my mother should be kind enough to tell me about him.

A mother is a special gift from God. There are those who seek these kinds of gifts. A father's love is the most important gift a father can offer to his child. A father needs to be there for his child, to build the foundation for his child's life. A father, a father, a father. To know my father and enjoy his love was my chief desire.

On that day my mathematics teacher, Mr. Hope Kagabangi, called me to his office. He could see the resentment I had, but really didn't know what was bothering me. All he wanted to do was to offer a little help and nothing else.

"I've been watching you since last year", he said. "You seem to be in a very strange agony. Sometimes in my class you seem to be worried about something. My dear child, is there something wrong at home"?

"No, sir. Everything is fine. I am just tired", I claimed.

"Tired"? he asked.

"Yes, tired. I guess it's because I study a lot".

I figured he would get off my back if he thought I was really hitting the books. Of course, I was so

The Darkest Secret of Life

distracted with my obsession about my father that I hardly studied at all.

"I haven't been impressed by any of your work this year, my dear. I suspect you are lying about your studying. I know teenagers meet different predicaments as they grow up, but you shouldn't let any of your troubles bring you down. I know you're a smart girl. You're not notorious, so whatever is troubling you, you should just let it go, my child", he advised.

"Yes, sir. Thank you so much", I replied although I wondered how he knew I was lying. Perhaps getting only 25 percent on that last test gave me away.

The flames of fire were settled down for only two weeks. Then they started again and this time I felt worse. I stopped studying altogether; I left my clothes and room messy; I spurned all offers of help. Even my mother could not stop me from acting this way.

"You're the reason why I behave this way", I told her. "If you could only find some generosity and tell me the truth about my father, mother"! I said rather plaintively.

"If you knew the truth and concentrated on it, I know you would never stop questioning me", she said. "I'd never hear the end of it".

The Darkest Secret of Life

Part of the problem in my mind was that we live in a village, not a huge metropolis. I'm sure that half the adults here know the details of my start in life. They know who my father is; they know if he has moved away, was sent to prison, was killed in some accident. I'm the only really interested person who is being kept in the dark.

People never stop talking. The rumours probably roam all over. Gossipers are never tired of talking about details they don't know. Feeling the buzz whenever I went anywhere got me down.

I went from being one of the smartest girls in my grade to being at the lowest end of the class. I wanted to pull myself up, but I couldn't. The situation drove me berserk. It deflected me from my studies. As days went on, I became more and more miserable and that really got my mother feeling sick with a guilty conscience.

My mother's every prayer was that God would help me to move on and forget about knowing my father. It seemed as though her prayer wasn't heard at all.

Mother decided to ask one of my friends to help.

"Maybe she will listen to you because you're the same age", she told Marianne.

The Darkest Secret of Life

"If she can't listen to me, perhaps she can listen to a young one", she thought.

My best friend tried to help.

"I've been talking to your mother for some time now, Clintashia", Marianne said. "She has been telling me of your behaviour. My dear friend, I've told you before and I am still telling you, your mother must have a good reason why she doesn't want to talk about the things from the past. Why can't you also let go of the past, huh? I am sure you're better off without your father. Why are you dragging your mother into such agony"?

Although that straight talk was just what I needed, I didn't see it.

"No! Hell no", I responded. "She's the one dragging me into agony. If only she could tell me the truth, nothing but the whole truth, then I would let go of the past".

"Well", Marianne said, "I've tried my level best. Oh yes, I did really try, but you can never banish the past. It seems to me that you're too keen on digging up the past. Suit yourself; it's your life", she concluded.

Marianne didn't give up on me as a friend. She simply realized that she was talking to someone who wouldn't listen and decided not to lose our

The Darkest Secret of Life

friendship over something that she couldn't control.

I kept on complaining to my mother without any result.

Poor mother continued to indulge me, but that did not mean anything to me. One night, when we had dinner together, mother tried to talk with me, but I wouldn't reply. I was actually distracted and unresponsive, whereas mother felt ecstasy deep inside her heart because for quite a long time we had not had dinner together.

My mother didn't lose hope. She always hoped for happiness in our house. She believed that someday things were going to be alright and we would be a happy family again.

The Darkest Secret of Life

Chapter Two

Although days, weeks and months passed, I didn't give up causing tumult and turmoil at home. I was becoming a bad person. I was killing myself and my mother slowly, but I did not recognise it because of the resentment I felt.

For a long time, mother tried to pull things together, but with no one's help she was not successful. She was becoming depressed. Eventually, she became very sick. Every night she would be writhing in pain, but even that did not change my mind. Death was knocking at my mother's door and she was desperate to let it come inside, but the thought of leaving me made her refuse the invitation.

She was getting worse every day. In the early hours of the morning one day, she asked me to accompany her to the hospital, but I refused.

"Please Clintashia, I'm begging you. I'm seriously in pain", she cried with a little voice.

"No, lady. Please do not ever consider me to be your daughter because if I were your daughter you wouldn't hide things from me. I refuse to accompany you to the hospital", I replied.

Eventually, mother had to call one of her colleagues to drive her to the Nkowankowa

The Darkest Secret of Life

Health Centre on Bankuna Street where she was admitted to the critical care ward. I wouldn't go there to see her. I acted totally nonchalantly as though my mother's condition was not my concern. I cared only about myself. This selfish behaviour ruined the good relationship I had with my mother.

Sadly, mother wasn't getting any better because she had no feelings of serenity. She really wanted and needed to be calm, but she continued to be anxious and upset. After three weeks in the hospital, instead of getting better she got worse every day and that worried her doctors. They tried to talk with me, but I refused to give them a chance.

A long-lost sister of mother's heard that she was in hospital and rushed there to see her. When she arrived and was told of her sister's predicament, she was not happy at all. She made an oath that she would do anything she could for her sister as long as she could stay there.

Having her sister there helped mother get better. At last, she received wise words, love and care that helped her move on.

Of course, I was still doing my own thing. For quite a long time, I had not gone to the hospital. My aunt tried by all means to talk to me, to make me understand and realise the importance of my

The Darkest Secret of Life

mother in my daily life, but I wouldn't accept any of my aunt's advice.

After another week, mother was discharged from the hospital. She was very happy to go home. When she and her sister arrived there, she started looking all around her house to see if things were the way she had left them. She found that everything was in its place and that made her happy.

That night, when she was taking a nap in her room, I went to see her. She was excited to see me.

"Mother"! I said very gently.

"Clintashia! How are you? I'm so glad to see you", she replied with the voice of love.

She had thought she would never talk with me again. She felt joy deep inside her heart.

"Mother, listen to me. I'm so sorry for all my wrongdoing. I never meant to hurt you as I did", I confessed.

Mother interrupted me.

"Shhh. It's okay my sweet bunny, really it's okay. I do not blame you. You had every right to be upset", she murmured.

The Darkest Secret of Life

Finally, I really showed some respect. I meant every word I was saying. The words bought joy and healing to my mother. Listening to wise words from me made her have second thoughts about her secrets. She considered telling me the truth about my father. On the other hand, she really wanted to protect me because she knew that if she told me the truth, people might try to intervene in our lives.

One moment she tried to speak the truth and the next her voice would shut down. She sat up until sunrise thinking of how she should approach me about it.

It was a quiet summer day when I woke up and prepared breakfast in bed for mother.

"Mmm, breakfast in bed. You really spoil me, honey. I am grateful", mother said.

Mother was really smiling. She was clearly elated and felt joy in her heart.

"I've been wondering all night what to tell you. I saw that it's been unfair of me to hide things from you. I've made up my mind to tell you the truth about your father", she said.

She was in tears.

I responded in a way that surprised mother.

The Darkest Secret of Life

"Oh mother, relax. Let the past be the past and the future be the future. Don't worry about anything anymore. I just hope that at some time when you are ready to tell me, I am going to know everything. Now stop worrying and be still in your soul. Be yourself, okay, mama"?

I finally realized that having a safe and healthy mother was more important to me than knowing whatever secrets mother was hiding from me about my father.

Mother wiped her tears and we cuddled in peace and harmony.

The Darkest Secret of Life

Chapter Three.

For the six months since we had reconciled, we enjoyed every second we spent together. The relationship of a mother to her daughter was now warmer than ever.

On Friday, mother decided to take me out to a restaurant where she could tell her me the truth about my father while we enjoyed a good meal.

"Mommy, I'm getting curious now. Tell me where we're going", I asked.

I was rather excited because I knew that mother was going to take me to one of the top class restaurants. We went to Karlo's where the meals were quite expensive.

We both had starters and the main course. When we were about to have dessert, mother spoke.

"Well, my young lady, it's been close to seventeen years that I've hidden this secret from you", she said.

I objected.

"No, mother. Not now, please. I'm not in the mood for that", I protested.

The Darkest Secret of Life

"You will never be ready for it", she said. "Besides that, you deserve to know the truth. You don't know how painful it is for me to hide this information from you, my closest love. I've made up my mind to tell you the truth tonight, now".

I started shivering as though I had been doused with cold water. I really wanted to stop mother, but I also wanted to know the truth. I was thirsty for the truth.

"Just promise me that you won't react badly after knowing the truth", mother asked politely.

I slowly nodded twice.

"It was September, 1998 when I went to see my mother in Pretoria. I was jovial about the trip. My uncle was taking me there. I had not seen my mother for a long time so my uncle suggested that we go there during the school holidays".

"We left here in the evening because we had to catch the last train. It was the following morning when we arrived. We went straight to my mother's apartment. We found her cleaning. She did not go to work that day because she..."

I interrupted her again.

"Oh come on, mother. You're taking too much time. Just get straight to the point. I've been

The Darkest Secret of Life

listening to your long story but I cannot connect the dots of how the story is related to my father. Are you sure you're still telling me about my father"? I asked.

"Yes. You have to listen to me attentively", mother requested.

"It's okay. I'll try to listen very carefully, Mommy".

"I was saying that my mother did not go to work that day. We found her cleaning. She was so happy to see me. Unfortunately, she had to rush to help her friend from Soshanguve".

"Help her with what"? I asked.

"She had to prepare lunch for her in-laws".

"Oh, I see".

I nodded.

"Yes. When she was gone, I went to buy bread at the nearest tuck shop. I met this tall, handsome guy with a cute smile. Plus, he had dimples. He waved goodbye to me and I waved back. I bought two loaves and went back home, I did not allow him to walk with me. I went alone. Mind you, at that time I was still a virgin. I did not want to

The Darkest Secret of Life

hear anything from boys. I respected myself a lot".

"Now,... that's what I do, Mommy".

Mother smiled and said "Hmmm".

She continued with the story.

"Anyway, my Mom came back late that evening. Although it was late, I was happy because she came back with delicious food".

"The following day when my mother went to work, I was alone in the house. In the afternoon, I decided to go to the tuck shop. Because Mama left me with a couple of rand, I went there to get fried chips. As I was approaching the shop, the very same guy from the previous day came to me with a big smile. Unexpectedly, he hugged me and said that he had thought he would not see me again".

"I didn't say a word; I just stared at him. I was told that boys from the city were dangerous. I was afraid of them. That's why I didn't say a word to him".

"Hey, are you deaf"? he asked me.

"I didn't answer him at all. He started telling me how much he loved me. Again I did not answer".

The Darkest Secret of Life

Tears dropped from her eyes. She kept quiet for about five minutes.

"Are you okay, mother"? I asked.

I was worried.

"No, I'm not okay, my daughter, but I'll be okay. Don't worry. The guy took advantage of me. He raped me. Trust me; I've never been so hurt like that in my life. I felt like a dirty slut. I even tried by all means to commit suicide, but I didn't succeed".

"Don't continue, Mommy", I said. "It's okay. Don't worry. Everything is going to be fine. I bless the day you met him because if it wasn't for him, I wouldn't be here today. Jehovah did it for a purpose. It's okay. Come here".

We cuddled!

The Darkest Secret of Life

Chapter Four

It was a hot winter day. The sun was up and very hot for the winter season. I was happy for the weather and that it was a school day.

"Mother"! I shouted from the bedroom.

I didn't want anything; I just wanted to check that mother was okay.

"My dear daughter, I'm okay. Lock the door for me when you get off to school".

"Okay, I'm off. Have a good day and take care", I called.

Off I went to school.

In the meantime, Mr. Kagabangi, the mathematics teacher realized that my problem was related to a desire to know my true heritage. He knew the story, of course, and wanted to call me and tell me the whole truth about my origin, hoping that would set me back on the right track. He was hesitant to do so because he was afraid that the news could affect me adversely. He sent for me when the bell rang and I ran immediately to his office.

This time I decided to take the initiative.

The Darkest Secret of Life

"I've noticed that you've been calling me in here lately and to be honest I do not like it", I said. "Don't get me wrong, but I think that some learners might misunderstand why you see me so often and start spreading lies about us. You know I don't like being the topic of gossip from the mouths of idiots".

"I know", the teacher said. "It's just that you're such a good girl and I get worried every time when you're sad. I want to see you happy at all times. Are you feeling alright, dear"?

I just nodded once and left the office.

Generally, I did not understand the intention of the teacher. This meeting got me thinking and curious to such an extent that after school I borrowed Marianne's phone and called home. I asked mother if she knew my mathematics teacher, Mr. Kagabangi.

Mother quickly changed the subject, made up an excuse to end the call and said she would have to talk with me later.

I started talking to myself.

"Hmm. I wonder if my Mom knows anything about my mathematics teacher. He seems to take more interest in me than the other teachers do. I bet that even if she knows she won't tell me.

The Darkest Secret of Life

Anyway, it's okay. I shouldn't bother her again. I know she loves me. I don't have to push her until she feels ready to tell me more".

Marianne interrupted my thoughts.

"Girl! I've been talking to you several times now. Are you okay"?

"Oh you were? Yes I'm fine. Sorry, I'm just tired. What were you saying"?

"I need help with these equations, but I see you're not in a good space. Don't worry. We can do them later".

"If you say so. Be sure to remind me because I might forget".

When school ended for that day, I went home and found mother lying on her bed. It wasn't that she was not well; she was totally fine.

"You're back"? mother queried. "I was beginning to wonder if you were coming home or if someone had kidnapped you".

"Ha ha ha! Oh come on, Mommy, I'm a big girl. You know something like that wouldn't happen to me. Besides that, I'm covered by the precious blood".

The Darkest Secret of Life

Mother cleared her throat.

"You called me. What were you saying? I couldn't hear you clearly", she said.

"Oh, about that? Ah, never mind. I was just checking to see if you were okay. I was worried about you. Well, I'm just glad you're okay".

"I'm okay. You must stop giving yourself hard times because of me. I'm a big lady. I'm fine and I'll always be fine. Okay"?

"Yes, mother. I will try not to stress anymore", I assured her.

She forced a smile, went to the kitchen and came back with tea.

"Uhm, Mommy, may I ask you something"?

"Yes, my baby, you're welcome".

"Do you by any chance know Mr. Kagabangi from our school? He teaches English and Mathematics. He stays in Medi Park. I don't know if he's married or if he has kids because..."

Mother dropped a glass that shattered on the floor. Her hands were shaking.

"I do know him..." she said.

The Darkest Secret of Life

"Why are you reacting this way, Mama"? I asked.

"You really gave me such a fright", she said. "I thought you wanted to tell me that you're having an affair with him or something crazy like that".

"No, no, no, no Mommy! It's not like that. It's just that he seems to care a lot about me. Every time when I look sad, he calls me to his office. I don't know; maybe I'm exaggerating, but I think he's over-protective towards me. I wonder why he chooses me out of the whole class. Maybe he's noticed that I haven't had a chance to call someone 'father' and he is trying to help", I suggested.

"Oh, you think so? That may be possible. Do you have his contact number or email address or anything to reach him"? mother asked.

"I have his email address because we once submitted our tasks via emails", I said.

I went to my bedroom and returned with the email address.

"Mommy, whoa! What do you want to tell him? Don't you say something heartless or rude? He's picking on me enough. He thinks I should do better in mathematics", I explained.

The Darkest Secret of Life

"Oh no. I just want to thank him for his loving kindness towards my daughter", mother claimed.

Later I learned that mother sent an email to Mr. Kagabangi requesting to see him. He agreed, even sending the address of a restaurant where they could meet.

The Darkest Secret of Life

Chapter Five.

The day finally arrived. Mother went to the restaurant, though she admitted later that she was nervous. She waited for him for about fifteen minutes. He was late; however he did show up.

"Oh, Hope, late as always," she said.

He took a deep breath and sat down.

"Sorry. I know you hate being late. Something came up just when I was about to go. How have you been? It's good to see you".

"How have I been? How have I been? How do you expect me to be when you're busy with my daughter"?

"Gloria, it's been a secret from her forever", he said.

"I can't live with it anymore", said mother. "I'm tired living a life full of lies. My daughter deserves to know the truth. Believe me; you don't know how it feels to be with a person under the same roof while you're busy hiding something from that very person".

"She's a grown girl and she'll soon be eighteen", said Hope.

The Darkest Secret of Life

Mother interrupted.

"Oh, so you've been keeping track? Wow...that's. ...well, I don't know...it's just...I'm surprised".

"I know it might sound very strange and awkward, but I think that a girl that age needs to know where she fits in the world. Every adult in the village knows her story. She is an adult now. I think she should be strong enough to know the truth".

Gloria wouldn't agree that easily. Her only problem was how to tell her daughter the truth about her father.

"I think I have a solution that both of us can agree on. It won't bring any problems to Clintashia or to the school", said mother.

"And what is the solution"? Mr. Kagabangi asked.

He opened his ears to hear mother's idea, but unfortunately it wasn't a good solution at all in his mind.

She smiled as she proposed the solution.

"I will take my daughter away to another school", decided my mother. "Then you won't have to

The Darkest Secret of Life

worry about her marks because you won't be teaching her anymore".

"So you think that's the best solution"? asked Mr. Kagabangi. "After that, what will happen? How long are you prepared to live your life keeping secrets from her"?

"I guess that's for the rest of my life, because I am not prepared to tell her the truth until I feel ready and I don't know if I'll be ready before I depart this life", replied mother.

"It's a pity that things will not go according to your will, Gloria", Mr. Kagabangi stated.

"How do you mean"? mother asked in a very rude way.

"What I'm trying to say is that I am going to tell my student the whole truth on Monday. For too many years she's been kept in the dark and like anyone else, she deserves to know her heritage. Everyone else knows her origin. It isn't good for her studies for her to be worrying about it all the time", said Mr. Kagabangi rather forcefully.

"You wouldn't dare do that, Hope Kagabangi", said my brave, but misguided mother.

The Darkest Secret of Life

"Oh, watch me, my lady. I wanted to make things easy for everyone, but it seems that you want to fix things in a difficult way".

He stood up to show that he was done talking. He did not have the patience to listen to what Gloria wanted to say anymore. He was really fed up with what the woman had just told him.

"I think we're done here. Get ready to answer each and every question your daughter will ask. Until I see you again, goodbye", he concluded.

He walked out of the restaurant and didn't look back.

Gloria was left very confused. She looked as though she had seen a ghost. She immediately took her phone and called me.

"Mother, you kept me worried. Where are you? I've been looking for you almost everywhere. Are you okay"? I asked.

"Shh. I'm fine, okay? I'll be with you in about ten minutes".

She rushed home. She couldn't stop thinking of the meeting to such an extent that she nearly caused an accident, but then she managed to arrive safely. She knew that Mr. Kagabangi was ready to tell me the truth the very next day.

The Darkest Secret of Life

"My baby, I'm back. One of my old colleagues took me out for lunch. I'm sorry I didn't tell you. It was a surprise", she lied.

"I'm glad that you're back and you're fine. That's what matters to me. I care a lot about you, you know. Anyway, how was the lunch"? I asked.

"Lunch?...Oh, lunch was okay...actually I had fun. There's something I want to discuss with you when you're free", she said.

"Oh? Something like what? I hope it's good news, because I'm not ready for bad news at all", I claimed.

"It's not bad, not that bad at all", she assured me.

"Oh well, my ears are all yours. Talk to me, Mommy", I said.

"I was thinking, now that you'll be doing grade 12 next year, I was thinking that it would be an advantage for you to go to one of the better schools for your last year. Which school would you prefer"? she asked.

That idea came out of the blue. I had no idea that she was thinking of sending me to a different school.

The Darkest Secret of Life

"Ahh, Mommy. I've been doing well in my school since grade eight and I'm getting over the problems I had this year. I don't see any reason for leaving. Why would I leave such a good school with such good teachers"? I asked.

This bit of gloss differed from the way my friends and I usually described our teachers, but I didn't want to leave my friends even if a new school happened to be better.

"Thing is, I want the best for you. I want you to have a bright future. There's one school in the Cape and it's. ..." she tried.

I interrupted.

"Cape? Why so far? It's obvious that I'm going to varsity after next year, so I would like to spend quality time with you next year. No, Mommy. I refuse. I won't allow that. I'm not going anywhere, It doesn't make sense. Why didn't you remove me from that school before this year? Why did I go to that school in the first place? You went there, didn't you"? I protested.

"You don't understand, dammit"!

Mother never swore so she was obviously worked up about this idea. I decided to try to ignore the whole idea.

The Darkest Secret of Life

"Well, make me understand, mother. You know what? Forget it. I'm off to bed", I said rather firmly and scooted off to my bedroom before she could give me another reason for the move.

Mother stood outside my bedroom door.

"My bundle of joy"! she called. "I'm so sorry. I didn't mean to shout at you. I really didn't mean to hurt you. I know I shouldn't have shouted. Forgive me. I promise, it'll never happen again, okay"?

I didn't bother to answer.

"I'll even understand if you do not answer me because I wronged you. I shouted at you for no reason. I'm sorry", mother called again.

I refused to reply and mother finally went to bed where she tried to go to sleep.

The following day when I went to school, Mr. Kagabangi could not wait any longer. He fetched me from class and took me straight to his office.

"I know your mother wants to take you to another school", he said.

"What? How do you know that? Are you a prophet or something"? I asked.

The Darkest Secret of Life

"No, she just told me. I had lunch with her yesterday. She's trying to prevent you from learning the truth about your father and I want you to know the whole truth today. Do you know why"? he asked .

"Sir, I'm really confused. What are you on about"?

"Now sit down so you can understand me very well", he said.

As I was about to take a seat, my mother barged into the office. I was completely dumbfounded.

"What the?...mother?? What are you doing here? Why did you come? Is there anything wrong"? I asked.

Mother didn't answer. Instead she turned to my teacher and said "I knew you were going to do this because you're capable of anything. Why do you want to keep on hurting me? Aren't you tired from the past"? she asked.

"He hurt you before"? I asked. "What's going on here"?

"My dear girl", Mr. Kagabangi said. "Your mother and I had not been fair to you for about seventeen years now. We've been hiding the truth from you in the name of protecting you".

The Darkest Secret of Life

"Enough said now"!! I almost shouted. "Come on, talk to me. What truth are you talking about? What's hidden from me? Mommy why are you crying? This is getting on my nerves. What's going on"? I wanted to know.

"I'm your father", claimed my mathematics teacher. "That's what we have hidden from you. Oh yes, I am", he said.

There was a moment of silence. I couldn't say anything except to turn and look at mother hoping to hear her say that it's a lie.

Then mother confessed.

"I'm afraid it's true. He's your father", she admitted.

I collapsed.

The Darkest Secret of Life

The Darkest Secret of Life

About the Publisher

William Jenkins is a retired computer guy who took up writing mystery-adventure stories for middle school children, age 9 to 12. By self-publishing the eight stories using Amazon's Createspace system, he became familiar with the ease of publishing and has now published ten other books for friends and relatives.

William was contacted by Jackie Mukhawana, a secondary school student in Tzaneen, South Africa and together they produced an anthology of plays, stories and poems written by Jackie and his friends.

Sheilah learned about the project and sent in her story.

If you happen across this publication and are interested in having your writing published, send a sample of the writing to the publisher using email address williamhenryjenkins@gmail.com. There is no charge for this service.

The Darkest Secret of Life

www.ingramcontent.com/pod-product-compliance
Lightning Source LLC
Chambersburg PA
CBHW061003050426
42453CB00009B/1233